Our Part of the World

By Carmel Reilly

Pearson Australia
(a division of Pearson Australia Group Pty Ltd)
707 Collins Street, Melbourne, Victoria 3008
PO Box 23360, Melbourne, Victoria 8012
www.pearson.com.au

First published 2014 by Pearson Australia
2018 2017 2016
10 9 8 7 6 5 4 3 2

Publisher: Dian Faulisi
Project Manager: Tamara d'Mello-Pirois
Editor: Margaret Trudgeon
Cover and Series Designers: Jenny Grigg and Anne Donald
Designer: Norma van Rees
Copyright and Pictures Editor: Katy Murenu
Mac Operator: Rob Curulli
Illustrator: Fiona Lee
Printed in Australia by the SOS Print + Media Group

ISBN 978 1 4860 0854 4
Pearson Australia Group Pty Ltd ABN 40 004 245 943

Acknowledgements
We would like to thank the following for permission to reproduce copyright material.
The following abbreviations are used in this list: t = top, b = bottom, l = left, r = right, c = centre.

Alamy: Thomas Cockrem, p. 17r; Rob Walls, p. 7.
Corbis: Paul Harris, p. 25r.
Fotolia: pp. Cover, 1, 3, 4, 5, 10(all), 11, 12tr, 13(all), 14(all), 17b, 18, 19(all), 21b, 22, 24tl, 25bl, 28, 29(all), 30, back cover.
Getty Images: Kevin Clogstoun, p. 21r; Jeoffrey Maitem, p. 26; Sonny Tumbelaka, p. 15.

Every effort has been made to trace and acknowledge copyright. However, if any infringement has occurred, the publishers tender their apologies and invite the copyright holders to contact them.

Disclaimer

Some of the images used in *Our Part of the World* might have associations with deceased Indigenous Australians. Please be aware that these images might cause sadness or distress in Aboriginal or Torres Strait Islander communities.

Contents

Australia and Asia

Australia sits at the very edge of the region of Asia, just a few hundred kilometres south of Indonesia. Ties between Australia and Asia have existed for a long time; however, it has only been in the last 50 years or so that they have begun to grow and strengthen to such a great extent.

Today Australia has a lot to do with many countries in Asia through immigration, trade, tourism and aid. But, more than that, the countries of Asia are some of our closest neighbours. Getting to know and understand the countries and cultures that make up this vast and varied area is central to building strong, helpful relationships. In turn, these relationships will help to lead us into a happy and prosperous future.

Understanding the cultures of our neighbours helps to build strong relationships.

LET'S FIND OUT

- In what ways is Australia connected to Asia?
- What are the four main areas of Asia?
- What kind of physical environments can be found in Asia?
- What are some of the traditions, languages and religions that are practised in Asia?
- What are the differences and similarities between Australia and countries in Asia?

The region of Asia is close to Australia.

Find your place

Asia is the world's largest **continent**. It extends from Turkey in the west to Japan in the north-east, Indonesia in the south-east, and Sri Lanka in the south. Australia lies just a few hundred kilometres across the sea from South-East Asia.

We are here!

Australia is an island continent in the Southern **Hemisphere**. It is part of Oceania, which includes the Pacific Islands and New Zealand. Its closest neighbours, just to the north, are Papua New Guinea, East Timor and Indonesia.

Australia is large and flat with only a few low mountain ranges and few major rivers. Its climate is a mix of tropical, temperate and desert.

Because the land in the centre of the country is desert or semi-desert, most farming occurs within a few hundred kilometres of the coast. This, and the fact that Australia's major cities are also on the coast, means that today over 80 per cent of its 23 million people live within 50 kilometres of the sea.

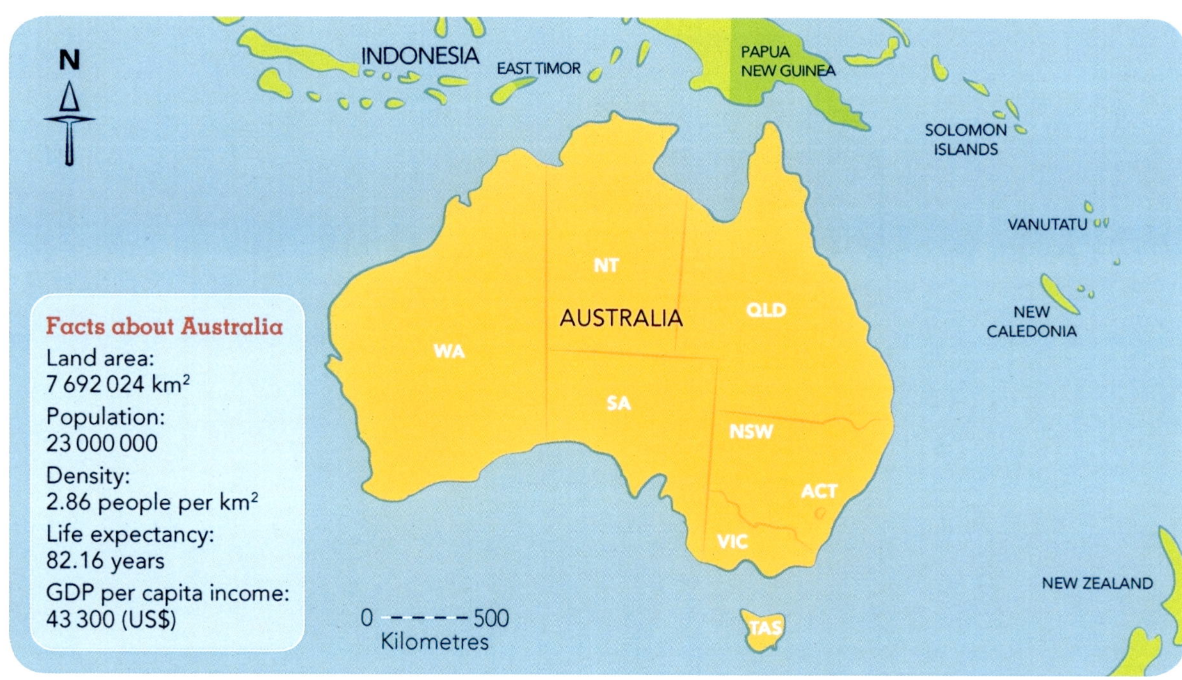

Map of Australia, showing how close it is to South-East Asia

Asian ties

Following British settlement in 1788, Australia looked to Britain for most of its immigration and trade, but after World War II Australia started to open up to the rest of the world. **Economic** ties were strengthened with Asia in the 1950s when schemes like the Colombo Plan (designed to promote economic development in Asia and the Pacific) and the Australian-Japan Trade Agreement were put in place. The arrival of **refugees** from Vietnam in the 1970s signalled the beginning of increased Asian migration to Australia.

Today Australia has strong connections with Asia. Increased migration from the Asia region means that 12 per cent of Australians now have an Asian background. Asian countries are among Australia's biggest trading partners. Australia takes part in a number of economic and **political** organisations that bring together countries in Asia, as well as the Pacific. These include the East Asia Summit (EAS) and the Asia-Pacific Economic Cooperation (APEC) Forum. Australia is also a part of the Asian Football Federation, the body that represents soccer across all of Asia.

Twelve per cent of Australian migrants come from the Asia region.

Asia

Asia covers about 30 per cent of the land surface of the world. It is bordered by Europe and Africa in the west and the Pacific Ocean in the east. It contains a wide range of environments ranging from deserts to jungles, mountains to grasslands. Due to its size it has a variety of climates – from cool, **temperate** climates in the north, that feature cold winters and hot summers, to hot-wet tropical climates, and hot-dry desert climates.

The highest and lowest places on Earth are in Asia. It has more mountains than any other continent, including the world's highest mountain, Mount Everest, on the Nepal–Tibet border, 8850 metres above sea level. The world's lowest-lying land is the shore around the Dead Sea, between Israel and Jordan, at 424 metres below sea level.

Asia has hundreds of rivers, which provide water for its huge population, as well as farming and industry. Rivers are also major transport routes for people and goods.

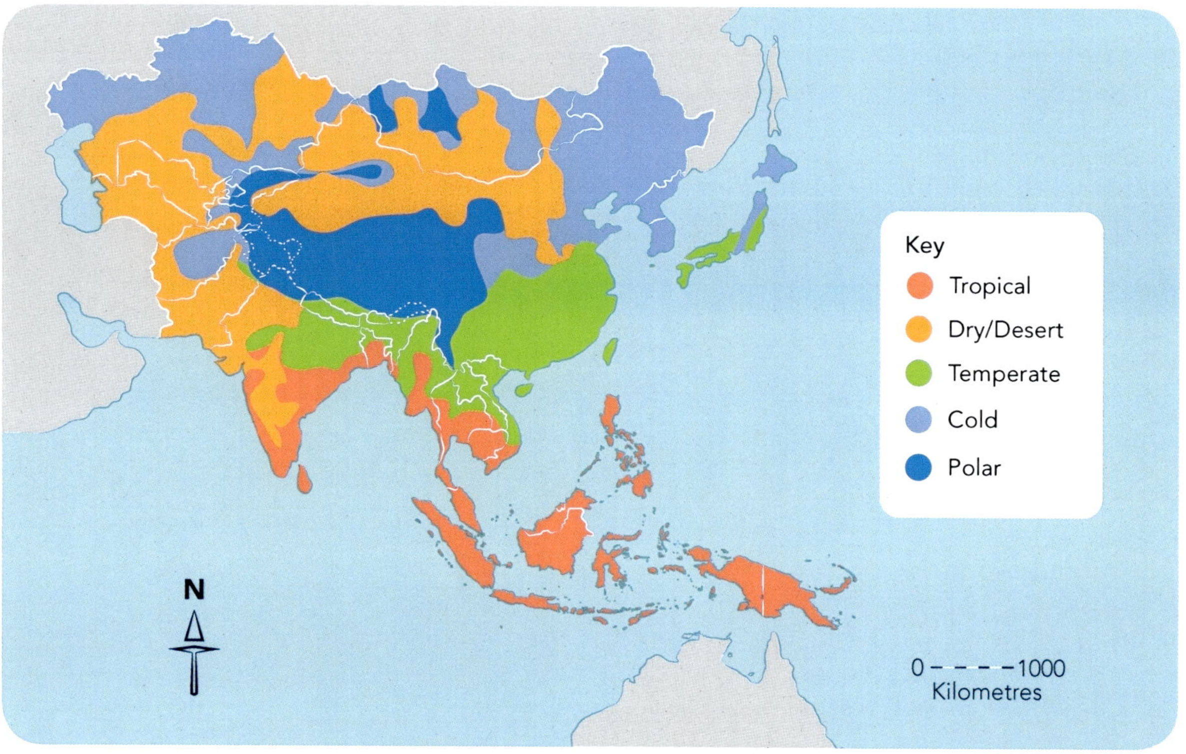

Map of Asia showing different climate zones

Many places, many peoples

Asia is not just the largest continent in area in the world, it also has the most people. Its 51 countries are home to more than 4 billion people – more than a half of the world's population. It was estimated in 2013 that the largest populations were around 1 360 000 000 in China and around 1 260 000 000 in India, making these countries not only the largest in Asia, but in the world. Other places, such as Bangladesh, Hong Kong, Singapore and Java in Indonesia, are also very densely populated. In 2013, the seven largest **urban** populations in the world were in Asia.

Asia is made up of many different **ethnic** and religious groups and its people speak thousands of different languages. Some countries, like Japan and Korea, have one main language and are made up of very similar ethnic and religious populations. Other countries, like China and India, have a wide range of different groups and languages.

Did you know?

In India, there are 780 languages. Thirty-eight different languages are spoken in the state of Bengal alone.

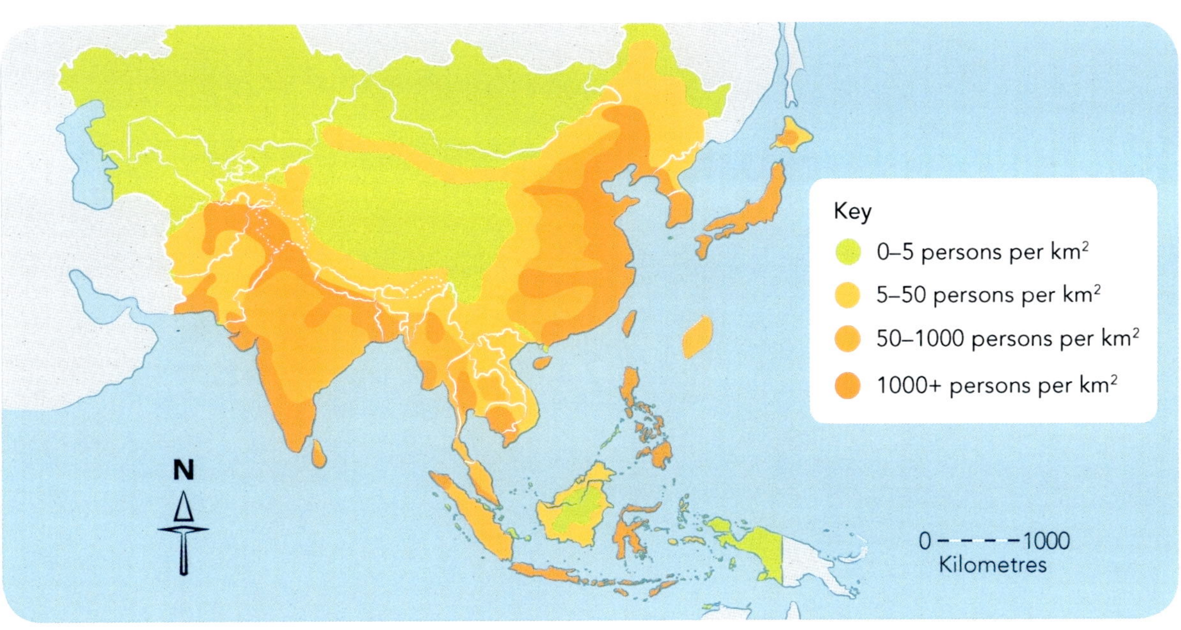

Map of Asia, showing population density

North-East Asia

China, Mongolia, North and South Korea, Japan and Taiwan are the countries that make up North-East Asia. Together, they account for 30 per cent of the area of Asia and contain about 38 per cent of Asia's population.

The environment

Mountain ranges and highlands can be found throughout North-East Asia. In China, the mountains and high **plateaus** in the centre of the country rise up to the Himalayas in the south-west. In Korea, Taiwan and the islands of Japan, coastal plains surround mountainous interiors.

A rice field in Guilin, China

North-west China and Tibet are made up of large areas of desert plateaus. China has many long slow-flowing rivers, while those of Korea and Japan tend to be short and swift.

The climate of the region varies from a **humid** cool **Continental climate** in the north to a humid subtropical climate in the south. Much of the area is affected by **monsoons**, winds that bring summer rain. Mongolia and western China have harsh, cold climates. The vegetation ranges from dry grasslands in the northern areas of China and Mongolia to temperate forests in the south of China, Japan and Taiwan.

The people

There are about 1.5 billion people in North-East Asia, accounting for around one-fifth of the world's population. China and Japan are two of the most densely populated countries in the world.

Tokyo is the largest city in the world.

Most of the people in North-East Asia live near coasts and rivers, where the land is suitable for farming and food supplies are close by. Rivers and the sea also provide easy transport for people and goods. In China, 92 per cent of the people are part of an ethnic group called the Han. The other 8 per cent belong to 55 different ethnic groups. In Japan, 99 per cent of people belong to the same ethnic group and speak Japanese. The situation is similar in Korea.

Increasingly, North-East Asians live in cities. South Korea has the highest number of people living in urban areas, while Japan's capital, Tokyo, with a population of 35 million, is the largest city in the world.

Did you know?
North-East Asia is about one and a half times the size of Australia, but has 68 times as many people!

Country	Capital	Area (km²)	Population (2013 est.)	Density (km²)	Life expectancy	Per capita GDP $US (2012)
China	Beijing	9640011	1349585838	138	74.99	9300
Japan	Tokyo	377930	127253000	337	84.19	36900
Mongolia	Ulaanbaatar	1564100	3226500	2	68.95	5500
North Korea	Pyongyang	120538	24720000	198	69.51	1800
South Korea	Seoul	100210	48955200	500	79.55	32800
Taiwan	Taipei	36188	23299700	639	79.71	39400

Source: *CIA The World Factbook*

Focus in on South Korea

South Korea is on the Korean **Peninsula** and is surrounded on three sides by sea. Its only land border is with North Korea. Its other closest neighbours are China and Japan.

Most of the large forests and rivers are in the west of the country, while the East has many sandy beaches.

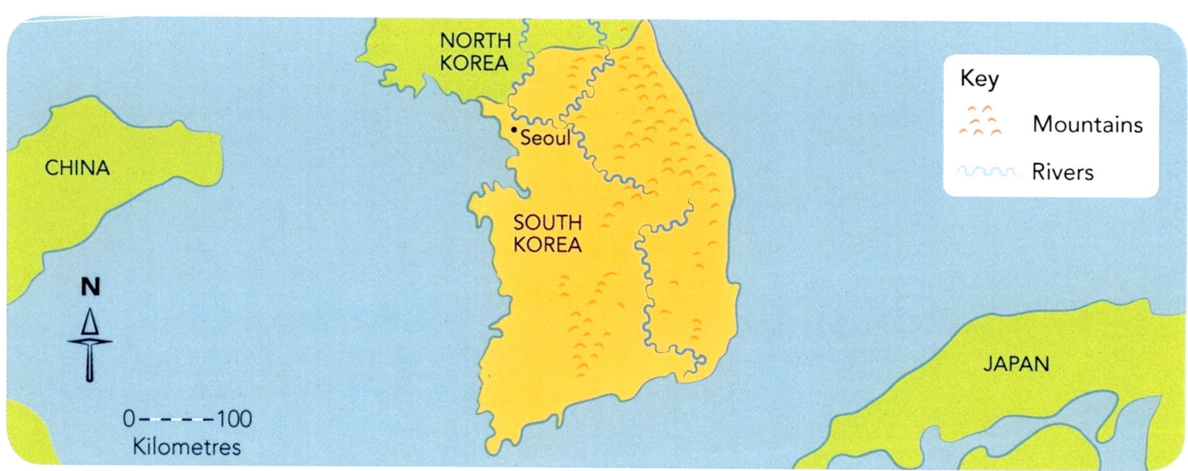

Topographical map of South Korea

At a glance

Area: 100 210 km^2

Comparative size in world: 109

Geographic coordinates: 37° 00′ N, 127° 30′ E

Climate: temperate, with the heaviest rainfall in summer. Temperatures in Seoul range from an average of –5°C in winter to an average of about 25°C in summer.

Physical environment: mostly hills and mountains with wide coastal plains in west and south

Arable land (land that can be farmed): 15%

Population: 48 955 203 (est. July 2013)

Comparative size in world: 26

Population density: 490 people per square kilometre

Urban population: 83.2%

Capital: Seoul, population 9.4 million

Life expectancy: 80.62 (2012)

GDP per capita income: US$32 800

Ethnic groups: 99.9% Korean

Language: Korean

Religion: none 43.3%, Christian 31.6%, Buddhist 24.2%, other or unknown 0.9%. Many Koreans also practise Confucianism

Source: *CIA World Factbook*

My life in a day

My name is Su-Jin and I live with my family in Seoul in an eighth-floor apartment. As well as my parents and my sister, Yu-Ri, my grandmother also lives with us. She moved from the country to stay with us after Grandfather died.

My day is busy in this big city. I leave for school at 8 a.m. by bus to get there just before 9 a.m. We have different lessons every day – such as maths and Korean, or science and English. Lunch is provided at school. My job at lunchtime is to set the table for the younger students. Other students have jobs serving and cleaning up.

When school finishes at 3 p.m. I take a sport class, like Tae Kwondo, a music class or extra lessons. Then I take a bus home through the busy traffic, arriving about 5.30 or 6 p.m. – just before dinner. My father, who has a job with a big company, often works late and can't join us. After dinner, I do homework for a couple of hours before I go to bed.

A view of Seoul, South Korea

South-East Asia

South-East Asia is made up of 11 countries and covers an area of 4 066 300 square kilometres – just a little more than half the size of Australia. It is home to over 610 million people.

The environment

The region is made up of two parts, mainland South-East Asia and island South-East Asia. Myanmar, Laos, Cambodia, Thailand, Vietnam and most of Malaysia, are part of the mainland. Singapore, Brunei, the Philippines, Indonesia, Timor Leste and parts of Malaysia are made up of over 20 000 islands.

Mountains feature throughout the whole area. In the Philippines and Indonesia, many of these are volcanic. A number of large rivers on the mainland provide food and transport, as does the sea that surrounds the islands.

The climate varies from a highlands climate in the mountainous areas of Myanmar, Indonesia and Malaysia, to the tropical rainforest that covers much of Vietnam, Malaysia and Indonesia. Tropical savannah is also common on the mainland, in Laos, Cambodia and Myanmar. Monsoon winds bring high rain between May and September to areas above the equator, and between October and April to those below.

Bromo Mountain Volcano, in Tengger Semeru National Park, Indonesia

The people

South-East Asia is home to hundreds of ethnic, cultural and religious groups, and its peoples speak nearly 1000 different languages. Islam is the major religion in the region, but there are also high numbers of Buddhists and Christians. **Confucianism** is also popular, especially among the Chinese who have settled throughout this part of Asia.

Traditionally, agriculture has been central to South-East Asian societies. The minerals found in volcanic soils, coupled with a wet, tropical climate in the islands, make much of the land excellent for farming.

An Indonesian farmer harvests rice in Central Java.

These days, about 42 per cent of the region's people live in cities. Jakarta, Manila and Bangkok are among the largest cities in the world. Population growth has been rapid in this part of the world, and it has doubled since 1970.

Country	Capital	Area (km^2)	Population (2013 est.)	Density (km^2)	Life expectancy	Per capita GDP $US (2012)
Brunei	Bandar Seri Begawan	5765	415710	74	76.57	55300
Cambodia	Phnom Penh	181035	15205000	84	63.41	2400
Indonesia	Jakarta	1904569	251160000	127	71.9	5100
Laos	Vientiane	236800	6695000	28	63.14	3100
Malaysia	Kuala Lumpur	329847	29628000	87	74.28	17200
Myanmar	Nay Pyi Taw	676000	63672000	92	65.6	1400
Philippines	Manila	300000	105720600	320	72.21	4500
Singapore	Singapore	724	5460000	7285	84.07	61400
Thailand	Bangkok	513120	67488000	125	74.05	10300
Timor Leste	Dili	14874	1172000	74	67.06	10000
Vietnam	Hanoi	331210	92477000	270	72.65	3600

Source: *CIA The World Factbook*

Focus in on Indonesia

Indonesia is an **archipelago** made up of around 15 000 islands scattered across the sea from Malaysia to Papua New Guinea. It has the fourth largest population in the world.

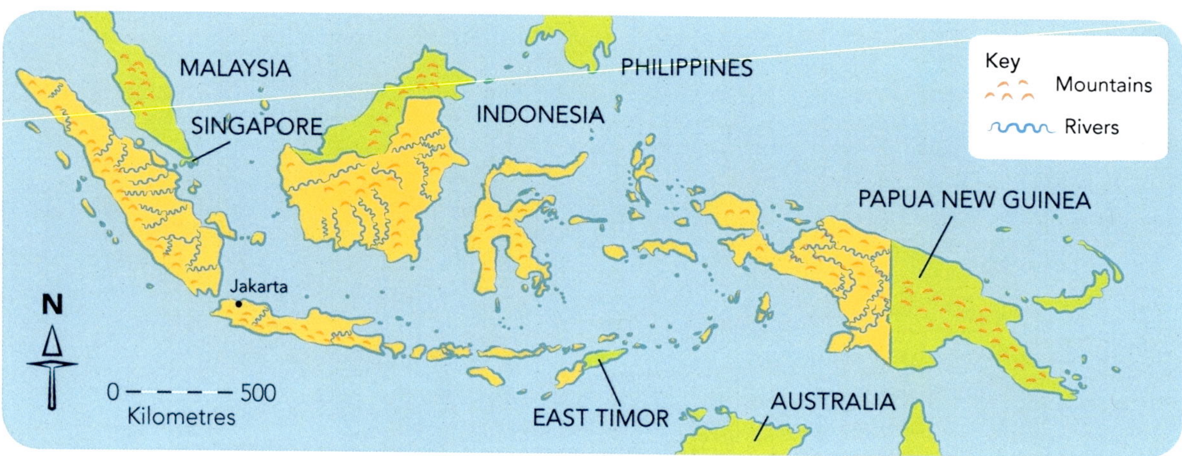

A topographical map of Indonesia

At a glance

Area: 1 904 569 km^2

Comparative size in world: 15

Geographic coordinates: 5° 00′ S, 120° 00′ E

Climate: tropical (hot and humid), but more moderate in the highland areas. Temperatures in Jakarta sit between 30°C and 32°C all year. Rainfall is highest in January and lightest from June to October.

Physical environment: coastal plains with mountains in the centre

Arable land (land that can be farmed): 12.34%

Population: 251 160 124 (est. July 2013)

Comparative size in world: 4

Population density: 131 people per square kilometre

Urban population: 50.7%

Capital: Jakarta, population 9.121 million

Life expectancy: 69.47 (2012)

GDP per capita income: US$5110

Ethnic groups: Javanese 40.6%, Sundanese 15%, Madurese 3.3%, Minangkabau 2.7%, Betawi 2.4%, Bugis 2.4%, Banten 2%, Banjar 1.7%, other 29.9% (2000 census)

Language: Bahasa Indonesia, English, Dutch, many local dialects

Religion: Muslim 86.1%, Christian 8.7%, Hindu 1.8%, other 3.4% (2000 census)

Source: *CIA World Factbook*

A trip to the country

I'm Arti, and I live in Jakarta with my parents and two brothers. Last week we went to visit my grandparents, who live in a small village near Batu in East Java – almost 700 kilometres away. We flew to Malang, and then took a bus to Batu. Even though it's a long journey, I love coming here. The air feels so fresh compared with the city and, because we are in the hills it is a tiny bit cooler than in Jakarta.

My grandparents' house is on a hillside and looks out across the lush, green valley to Mt Butak. A lot of the hillsides are terraced for agriculture, and the area is famous for growing apples. In the other direction, but luckily further away, is the famous Mt Bromo, a volcano that is still active! My grandfather said when it erupted a few years ago the sky was dark and the air was filled with ash.

There are lots of things to do here. There are waterfalls and ruins of ancient temples to see and a zoo, a museum and an eco park to visit.

Mt Bromo, Indonesia

South Asia

South Asia is set in a diamond shape between the Himalayan mountain range to the north and the Indian ocean to the south. Its eight countries cover an area of 4 480 000 square kilometres, or about 10 per cent of Asia. Its 1.7 billion people make up 34 per cent of Asia's population.

The environment

South Asia is dominated by mountains. Bhutan and Nepal are both in the Himalayas, as are parts of India, Pakistan and Afghanistan. Afghanistan, Pakistan, India and Sri Lanka also have their own central mountain ranges and large areas of rugged hills.

Vast areas of desert cover north-western India and southern Pakistan, while much of Bangladesh is low-lying coastal plain. Rivers are important everywhere, providing water for farming as well as transport across the country.

Climates in the region range from tropical and subtropical in Bangladesh and on the west coast of India and Sri Lanka, to cold highland climates in the mountainous parts of Afghanistan, Pakistan, Nepal and Bhutan. Most of the area is very hot and dry, and relies on monsoons to bring much needed summer rain for agriculture.

South Asia is dominated by mountains.

The people

South Asia is home to 20 per cent of the world's population and is the most densely populated area on the planet. In the region, five cities – Delhi, Karachi, Mumbai, Kolkata and Dhaka – are in the top 20 most-populated urban areas in the world. Although many of its people now live in cities, more than 70 per cent of the total population lives in the countryside.

South Asia is also one of the most **diverse** areas in the world. It is home to more than 2000 different ethnic groups, hundreds of different language speakers and many different religions. Hinduism is the largest of these, with more than 900 million Hindus in India alone. In Afghanistan, Pakistan, Bangladesh and the Maldives, Islam is the main religion, while in Bhutan and Sri Lanka most people are Buddhists.

Did you know?

With 1.21 billion people, India is the most **populous** country in the region. It also has a young population, with more than half of its citizens under 25 years old.

Country	Capital	Area (km²)	Population (2013 est.)	Density (km²)	Life expectancy	Per capita GDP $US (2012)
Afghanistan	Kabul	652 230	31 108 000	52	50.11	1 100
Bangladesh	Dhaka	147 570	163 654 015	1 099	70.36	2 100
Bhutan	Thimphu	38 394	725 000	18	68.44	6 800
India	New Delhi	3 287 240	1 220 800 359	382	67.48	3 900
Maldives	Malé	298	393 988	1 330	74.92	9 400
Nepal	Kathmandu	147 181	30 430 080	200	66.86	1 300
Pakistan	Islamabad	796 095	193 238 000	225	66.71	2 900
Sri Lanka	Sri Jayawardenepura Kotte	65 610	21 657 648	319	76.64	6 200

Source: *CIA The World Factbook*

Focus in on Sri Lanka

Sri Lanka is a large tropical island situated near the south-east coast of India.

A topographical map of Sri Lanka

At a glance

Area: 65 610 km^2

Comparative size in world: 122

Geographic coordinates: 7° 00′ N, 81° 00′ E

Climate: tropical (hot and humid); temperatures in Colombo range from 28°C to 31°C, but it is cooler in the highlands. There are two monsoon seasons – the north-east monsoon from December to March and the south-west monsoon from June to October.

Physical environment: coastal plains with mountains at the southern part of the centre

Arable land (land that can be farmed): 18.29%

Population: 21 675 648 (July 2013 est.)

Comparative size in world: 58

Population density: 330 people per square kilometre

Urban population: 15.1%

Capital: Colombo pop 753 000

Life expectancy: 76.15 (2012)

GDP per capita income: US$6200

Ethnic groups: Sinhalese 73.8%, Sri Lankan Moors 7.2%, Indian Tamil 4.6%, Sri Lankan Tamil 3.9%, other 0.5%, other 10% (2001 census)

Language: Sinhala 74%, Tamil 18%, other 8% English is often used

Religion: Buddhist 69.1%, Muslim 7.6%, Hindu 7.1%, Christian 6.2%, other 10% (2001 census)

Source: *CIA World Factbook*

Driving across my island

I am Roshan. My father works as a driver and takes tourists all around Sri Lanka in his car. A few times I have gone with him, which means I get to see some amazing parts of the island. We live in Colombo, which is the largest city in Sri Lanka, on the south-west coast. My father often drives people to some of the area's famous beaches and seaside towns, such as Galle, which was built by the Portuguese in the 1500s and added to by the Dutch in the 1600s. (Sri Lanka was colonised by the Portuguese, Dutch and British at different times.)

We have also gone to Kandy, which is up in the hills in the centre of the country. Kandy is a very ancient and beautiful place centred around a lake. There are lovely gardens and temples, and visitors can go on treks to see caves and waterfalls, or visit the nearby tea plantations. In August there is a big Buddhist festival called Esala Perahera, with dancing, drumming and parades of elephants.

Kandy, Sri Lanka

West Asia

West Asia is also known as the Middle East. It is a 6 255 160 square kilometre area – a little smaller than the size of Australia – wedged between South Asia, Europe and Africa. The 18 countries that make up this region have a combined population of 313 428 000.

The environment

Deserts, mountain ranges and large rivers are the strongest features of the West Asian environment. Apart from the areas that border seas and rivers, much of this part of Asia is arid (dry). The Arabian peninsula is mostly desert with some large rugged mountain ranges. Parts of Iran and Iraq are similar. The desert climate is very harsh, with little rain and temperatures that frequently reach 49°C, even in the shade. In Turkey and south and west Iran, grasslands are more common.

Desert and steppe climates are the most common throughout the area. A Mediterranean climate is found around the shores of the Mediterranean, Black and Caspian seas and at the head of the Tigris and Euphrates rivers.

The Oman desert, one of many in West Asia

Parts of Georgia have a humid subtropical climate.

The people

The people who live in West Asia are as varied as its climate. The main ethnic and language-speaking group throughout the Arabian Peninsula and in Jordan, Syria, Lebanon and Iraq are Arabs. The next largest groups are Turks, who speak Turkish and Iranians, who speak Farsi.

Other significant groups are Hebrew-speaking Jews in Israel, Pashto-speaking Afghanis, Armenians, Georgians and Azerbaijanis. The main religion is Islam, although the Jewish faith is represented in Israel and the people of Georgia and Armenia are largely Christian.

Large numbers of the region's people live around seas, lakes and rivers, where the weather is warmer and food can easily be grown. There are also many people living in large cities. Iran and Turkey are the most populous countries and their largest cities, Tehran and Istanbul, have populations of almost 14 million people each. The population density is lower here than in other parts of Asia and urbanisation is generally high, with countries like Kuwait and Qatar having more than 98 per cent of people living in cities.

Country	Capital	Area (km^2)	Population (2013 est.)	Density (km^2)	Life expectancy	Per capita GDP $US (2012)
Armenia	Yerevan	29 800	2 974 200	108.4	73.75	5 900
Azerbaijan	Baku	86 600	9 590 000	105.8	71.76	10 700
Bahrain	Manama	665	1 281 300	1646.1	78.43	29 200
Georgia	Tbilisi	69 700	4 555 900	68.1	77.51	6 000
Iran	Tehran	1 648 195	79 853 000	45	70.62	13 300
Iraq	Baghdad	438 317	31 858 400	73.5	71.14	7 200
Israel	Jerusalem	20 770	7 707 000	365.3	81.17	32 800
Jordan	Amman	89 342	6 482 000	68.4	80.30	6 100
Kuwait	Kuwait City	17 820	2 695 300	167.5	77.46	40 500
Lebanon	Beirut	10 452	4 131 580	404	75.46	16 000
Oman	Muscat	212 460	3 154 000	9.2	74.72	29 600
Qatar	Doha	11 437	2 042 400	123.2	78.24	103 900
Saudi Arabia	Riyadh	1 960 582	26 939 500	12	74.58	31 800
Syria*	Damascus	185 180	22 457 000	118.3	75.14	5 100
Turkey	Ankara	783 562	80 694 400	94.1	70.03	15 200
United Arab Emirates	Abu Dhabi	82 880	5 473 900	97	76.91	49 800
Yemen	Sana'a	527 970	25 408 200	44.7	64.47	2 300

*Note: Per capita GDP figure is for 2011.
Source: *CIA The World Factbook*

Focus in on Jordan

Jordan is located northwest of Saudi Arabia, between Israel and Iraq. The western side of Jordan has a Mediterranean climate and fertile ground, while in the east it is mainly desert.

Did you know?

Jordan is a landlocked country, except for 26 kilometres of shoreline along the Gulf of Aqaba, which opens into the Red Sea.

A topographical map of Jordan

At a glance

Area: 89 342 km^2

Comparative size in world: 112

Geographic coordinates: 31° 00′ N, 36° 00′ E

Climate: Mostly arid desert. There is a rainy season in the west from November to April

Physical environment: Mostly desert plateau (high plains) in the east, and highland areas in the west; The Jordan River and the Dead Sea separate Jordan from Israel.

Arable land (land that can be farmed): 1.9%

Population: 6 482 081 (July 2013 est.)

Comparative size in world: 105

Population density: 72.5 people per square kilometre

Urban population: 82.7%

Capital: Amman population 2 000 000

Life expectancy: 80.3 (2012)

GDP per capita income: US$6100

Ethnic groups: Arab 98%, Circassian 1%, Armenian 1%

Language: Arabic, English

Religion: Sunni Muslim 92% (official), Christian 6%, other 2% (2001 estimate)

Source: *CIA World Factbook*

My amazing land

My name is Samir and I live in Amman, which is Jordan's capital and largest city. My city is built on hills and I spend a lot of time walking up and down them as I go from my home to school, to friends' houses, to sport practice, or to the mosque. Sometimes when I look at all the white stone buildings jumbled together on the hillside I think that I might be back in ancient times because the city looks so old. But then I go over another hill and I see all the new buildings and the freeway, and it looks so modern.

One of the most incredible places in Jordan is the ancient city of Petra. Last year my school took a trip there. The long drive through the desert was rewarded when we reached the end and saw the amazing stone buildings.

People carved the huge city out of the hard desert rock 2500 years ago, and managed a vast water storage system, so they were able to survive here for more than 600 years.

Petra, Jordan

Good neighbours: our relationship with Asia

Australia is connected to Asia in many ways, including through aid, trade, education, tourism and defence alliances. Increasingly, we are becoming more personally connected through migration, with growing numbers of people from Asia settling in Australia.

Aid

Every year the Australian government gives aid to other countries that are in need of extra help. Most of this aid is to the Asia-Pacific region, an area that is home to two-thirds of the world's poor. Twenty countries in Asia, including Mongolia, North Korea, India, Afghanistan and Iraq, recieve help in areas such as health, education, economic and governmental development, as well as **humanitarian** aid, which is often given when there has been a crisis such as an earthquake or a drought.

Australian humanitarian workers travel the world to provide disaster relief wherever they are needed.

In Pakistan, for example, Australian aid has helped to train almost 9000 **midwives**, provided free textbooks for 1.5 million children and contributed to treating 50 000 people for eye diseases. Aid has also improved education for children in rural areas and provided work skills training – like carpentry and plumbing – for local people so they are able to improve their communities.

Trade

About 40 years ago Australia's main trading partner was Britain. Now it is China, with 24.6 per cent of our exports going to that country and 14.9 per cent of our imports coming from there. Australia's main exports to China are iron ore, coal, gold, copper, aluminium and crude petroleum, while the main imports are clothing, furniture, phone equipment and computers.

Exports to Japan and Korea, our next biggest Asian trading partners, are coal, minerals and beef, with imports of motor vehicles, refined petrol and engineering and phone equipment. Australia exports gold, copper and vegetables to its fourth largest trading partner, India, and imports pearls, gems, motor vehicles, medicines, iron and steel.

Another form of trade is in services and one of these is education, which is now Australia's fourth largest export. Asian students make up the bulk of students coming to Australia for both secondary school and higher education. Some Australian universities have also opened campuses in parts of Asia to service the rapidly growing population's demand for better education.

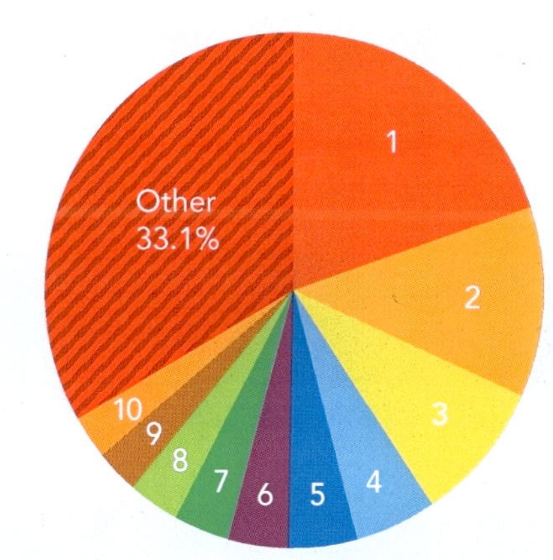

1 China 19.9%
2 Japan 11.9%
3 United States 8.9%
4 Republic of Korea 5.4%
5 Singapore 4.6%
6 United Kingdom 3.8%
7 New Zealand 3.5%
8 India 3.3%
9 Thailand 3.0%
10 Malaysia 2.6%

Source: Australian Government

Australia's top 10 two-way trading partners, 2011

Visiting

Tourism to Asia from Australia has grown since the 1970s. Once it was only backpackers who ventured to places such as India, Nepal and Thailand, but now these countries draw tourists from every walk of life and every age group. Communist countries, like China and Vietnam, which were once closed to foreigners, have opened their borders over the last 20 years and thousands of Australians now visit them every year. Indonesia is the most popular Asian destination for Australians, followed by Thailand and China.

Tourism traffic is not all one-way. For a long time, Japanese tourism was strong in Australia. Now, people from China are our most regular visitors from Asia, third in number behind New Zealanders and British. Large numbers of Asian tourists also continue to come from Japan, as well as South Korea, Singapore and Malaysia.

Did you know?

Since the year 2000 more than 26 million Asian visitors have come to Australia for holidays, to visit friends and relatives, to study, or to do business or work.

Asia is a popular tourist destination for Australians.

Moving to Australia

My name is Sana and I came to Australia from India with my family four years ago. It was hard to settle at first, until I began to realise that lots of people in my class were also from different countries and that made me feel better.

Living here is very different from where we lived in India. Our city, Mumbai, was very crowded. When I went outside there were always people everywhere and lots of noise. Here, we live in a suburb about 15 kilometres from the city centre. It is very quiet and the neighbour's house feels like it is a long way away!

We have been on holiday to Uluru. It was great to travel through the desert and experience the wide open spaces. Mostly, when you travel across the Indian countryside you can always see something – people, houses, animals, crops. Even though we have some desert areas in India too, there are still more people living near and around them. India is half the size of Australia but has 50 times more people!

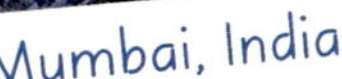

Mumbai, India

Connections

We are connected to Asia in so many ways – from trade and tourism to migration – and increasingly on a personal level through our schools, communities and families. As all of us travel more often and spend extended time in other countries, we have more to do with other people and other cultures. Some of us are lucky enough to be able to travel to places in Asia, like Bali, Singapore, Thailand or Hong Kong and see these countries and how the people there live.

But even if we don't travel, most of us will know people from Asia who have come here to live or work.

Getting to know our Asian neighbours is good for us and for them. We can learn about each other's history and culture and discover new ways of doing things and seeing the world. We can help each other when times get tough, and come to each other's aid in times of war or disaster. After all, isn't that what being a good neighbour is all about?

Australian children connect us to many different parts of the world, including Asia.

Glossary

archipelago a large group of islands

Confucianism religion based on the ideas of the ancient Chinese wise man, Confucius

continent one of the world's seven main areas of land (Europe, Asia, Africa, North and South America, Australia, Antarctica)

Continental climate the kind of climate found around a large body of land

diverse things that are very different from each other

economic related to trade, industry and the creation of wealth

ethnic a group with a common cultural tradition

hemisphere one-half of the world, divided into north or south at the equator, or midline around the Earth

humanitarian concerned with or seeking to help people, especially in times of disaster

humid when there is a lot of water vapour in the air

midwives people who are trained to help deliver babies

monsoons seasonal winds in South-East and South Asia, from south-west in May–September, bringing rain; then from north-east in October–April (dry)

peninsula a piece of land that projects out and is surrounded by water on three sides

per capita GDP a measure of the total output of a country; the gross domestic product (GDP) – the total amount of money a country makes – is divided by the number of people in the country

plateaus areas of flat high ground

political relating to a country's government

populous having a large population

refugees people who have fled their homeland to escape war

temperate mild temperatures

urban relating to a town or a city

Index